A.M. or P.M.
Devotionals for Men

William J. Krutza

BAKER BOOK HOUSE
Grand Rapids, Michigan

1 Let It Pour!

For as the rain and the snow come down from heaven, and return not thither but water the earth, making it bring forth and sprout, giving seed to the sower and bread to the eater, so shall my word be that goes forth from my mouth; it shall not return to me empty, but it shall accomplish that which I purpose, and prosper in the thing for which I sent it (Isa. 55:10, 11, RSV).

God wants something good to sprout within you. His Word is like rain, causing life to spring forth. He sends it to you, most often in short showers, for this good purpose. And you can be sure, as you let the biblical truths of this book soak into your soul, God is going to make His Word prosper in the things for which He sent it.

Lord, pour out from your Word those things which will make my life come alive and be productive in Your kingdom.

2 Our Incomparable God

O Lord, God of Israel, there is no God like thee, in heaven above or on earth beneath, keeping covenant and showing steadfast love to thy servants who walk before thee with all their hearts (I Kings 8:23, RSV).

Our God is incomparable. All other gods are of human invention; some are no more than carved blocks of wood. Our God is in a class all by Himself.

Idols, figments of the human imagination, personifications of idealistic characteristics are not our God! God is beyond men. That's why we can worship Him and commit ourselves to Him. He never lets us down; He keeps His promises. He shows His love to be steadfast and strong and always available.

It is great to bow before Him and say, "My Lord and my God!"

Though our minds are limited in trying to comprehend all You are and do, we worship You, Lord. Open our understanding to know and experience more of Your majesty.

3 Others Worth Xeroxing

Watch the upright and observe the righteous, for there is a future to the man of peace (Ps. 37:37, MLB).

We can either envy or emulate successful people. What better people can we emulate than those who do right? We need to take a good look at them—and a second look and a third or fourth. Especially notice those people who know how to get along with others, who live peaceably with fellow workers and neighbors. They are excellent examples to follow in a world of tension and personal pressures. They are worth xeroxing.

Give me the alertness of mind, O God, to discover people whose lives are worthy of my copying. Then give me an ambitious will to duplicate in myself those good characteristics I see in them.

4 Prize Winners

Do you remember how, on a racing-track, every competitor runs, but only one wins the prize? Well, you ought to run with your minds fixed on winning the prize! (I Cor. 9:24, Phillips).

Far too much of life, even beyond sports, is based on the concept of the one winner, the rest losers. The better philosophy is one or several winners, the rest competitors.

Today's runner-ups can be first-placers tomorrow. Don't count how many competitors you have, aim for the top spot yourself. Set high goals. Use your physical and mental abilities to full capacity.

Paul exhorted the Colossians, "Whatever your task is, put your whole heart and soul into it." That will produce a winner regardless of when you cross the finish line.

**Lord, give me the motivation
to be competitive,
the ability to set life-stretching goals,
and an unsatisfied spirit until I reach them.**

5 Wisdom's Starting Line

How does a man become wise? The first step is to trust and reverence the Lord! (Prov. 1:7, LB).

Where does one find wisdom's starting line? By reading the best-selling books? By listening to well-known university lecturers? By watching the latest TV documentaries?

Solomon said that wisdom comes by stopping for a moment to worship, to recognize and reverence God, to think about who He is and what He does.

Taking time out at the first part of the day is an excellent way to incorporate God's thinking into your thinking.

Lord, something happens inside of me when I contemplate Your majesty and mystery. Help me to understand more of the world's greatest truth: "The Word became flesh and dwelt among us."

6 The Weekday Mirror

Then God said, ''Let us make man in our image and likeness to rule the fish in the sea, the birds of heaven, the cattle, all wild animals on earth, and all reptiles that crawl upon the earth'' (Gen. 1:26, NEB).

Being like God makes us important. But that isn't the image we usually see in the mirror on Monday morning. Sure we might be a little more sanctimonious on Sunday. But come Monday morning with the rush hour traffic, a desk full of work, and fellow employees who wish the weekend was still here, can others—or can we—see the image of God in our lives? We need to take a good look at ourselves. Monday morning religion should come closer to Sunday morning religion!

Thank God, He wants His image to come through. That is why He keeps working with us.

Lord, may the way I take charge of my day give evidence of my being made by You and my being vitally connected to You.

7 Watch Your Steps

For the Lord knows the way of the righteous, but the way of the wicked will perish (Ps. 1:6, RSV).

Advice from an old-timer's almanac: Select your ruts in life with care. You'll walk in them for a long time.

A lot of people watch the ways of good people, and God does, too. He is interested in our plans and in the paths we take to accomplish them. The way of the wicked, however, doesn't get any positive treatment at all.

The way of the wicked is something like burning wood. It looks flashy and can attract considerable attention. But in the end it turns to ashes. Worse yet, it leads to eternal doom.

There are two ways I can live—the way of life in Christ or the way of death in evil and self-centeredness. Lord, give me the brains and willingness to choose what produces life—what is eternally as well as temporarily worthwhile.

8 Bread

Jesus answered, "It is written: 'Man does not live on bread alone, but on every word that comes from the mouth of God' " (Matt. 4:4, NIV).

Bread is a staple food throughout the world. Every man needs his share of food to stay alive.

But the center of life isn't the stomach. Men have souls which also need constant feeding.

This is why we read devotionals and study the Bible. We digest eternal truths and get acquainted with God. Tune yourself in to what He says to you personally. Feed well and feed often; your soul will never get too fat!

Lord, help me to realize the importance of both short devotional times and longer periods of Bible study. Help me to grasp more of Your precepts for successful living.

9 Loyalty

Never let go of loyalty and faithfulness. Tie them around your neck; write them on your heart (Prov. 3:3, GNB).

Sticking with someone or to some principle is loyalty. Practice loyalty and faithfulness to your marriage partner, to your business associates, and to political statesmen whom you believe in. Most of all, be loyal to God and His principles.

Don't be afraid to let your loyalty be seen. Tie it around your neck; get it out in the open. But have it inside as well. Write it on your heart!

Thank You for being loyal to me, O Lord, even when I don't reciprocate. Teach me the value of faithfulness to You and to my fellow human beings.

10 Character Testers

We can be full of joy here and now even in our trials and troubles. . . . these very things will give us patient endurance; this in turn will develop a mature character (Rom. 5:3, 4, Phillips).

True character often surfaces during times of trouble. Do you display frustration, rebellion, resentfulness, illogical thinking, erratic actions, or patience, kindness, understanding, level-headedness?

In times of leisure we display smiling faces. But pressures usually reveal our inner natures, who we really are. All that has been built into us, or that which is missing, shows up then! Trials and troubles can be character builders or revealers. It depends on what we are made of.

Give me the grace to react to troubles with true Christlikeness. Then I'll know what James meant when he said, "Count it all joy when you meet various trials."

11 Praying for Happiness

Fill all who love you with your happiness. For you bless the godly man, O Lord: you protect him with your shield of love (Ps. 5:11c, 12, LB).

God wants every man to be happy. But by the looks of many men, even Christian men, the message hasn't gotten through yet.

Those who love God can pray for happiness. He likes to make His children smile. He fills them with joy. Jesus said, "Ask and you will receive, so that your joy may be complete." Happiness comes to the praying man.

Lord, sometimes I'm grouchy.
Sometimes I'm sad and lonely.
Sometimes I pity myself.
Come and change all this!

12 The Good Old Days

Do not ask why the old ways were better than these; for that is a foolish question (Eccles. 7:10, NEB).

Nostalgia is great if it doesn't obliterate the reality of the now. Remember the good old days? Everyone over thirty remembers some of them. Many of the old ways are excellent and ought to be continued. But today is the most important day of your life. You can't relive the past; you can only recall it. You can't live the future; you can only plan for it. Today is really the only day you have to live. Build upon the past with an eye to tomorrow, but be sure to fill today to the brim.

Lord, my best memories are of Your forgiveness, and I have hope for my future because of Your grace. Today I will build on the foundation You have laid for me.

13 Personal Peace

I now leave you the blessing of peace, I give you the blessing of my own peace. I myself do not give it in the way the world gives it. Stop letting your hearts be troubled or timid (John 14:27, Williams).

Peace is one of life's most prized possessions. Men desire tranquility of mind. They desire peace within relationships—among friends, relatives, and fellow workers. They long for peace between nations. Greatest of all, they desire peace with God. That peace has been established for us through the dynamics of the death and resurrection of Jesus Christ and is made real by the Holy Spirit's indwelling. When one obtains this eternal peace with God, peace with men comes easier.

Lord, You promised peace. Make this a reality within and a testimony without as I rely on You.

14 The Warehouse of the Mind

Wise men store up knowledge, but the mouth of the foolish hastens ruin (Prov. 10:14, MLB).

The human mind is a warehouse to be packed full of useful knowledge, or to be emptied of its contents.

Some know the values of the storage process. They constantly study to gain new knowledge, to keep their minds alert.

Others seem to be in the shipping business until the warehouse is empty. They keep delivering empty cartons, not realizing the emptiness. There can be few worthwhile mental deliveries without an adequate filling of the warehouse of the mind.

Thank You, Lord, for giving me an alert and inquisitive mind. Help me sift the significant from the spurious. And when I talk, give me the instinctive wisdom to close my mouth before my mind runs dry.

15 Creative Goodness

Blessed are they who observe justice, who do righteousness at all times (Ps. 106:3, RSV).

Some claim they get bored doing good. For them, a little off-color living puts sparks into life. But they're just not looking in the right direction. Doing what's right can be creative and exciting. God proved that, as a peek at Genesis 1 reveals. He created everything and saw that it was all good.

There's no limit to constructive creativity, even by men. If you've become bored, try doing something special for others.

Lord, those who practice evil really aren't at ease. They will soon face the consequences of their living. I'd rather operate out of a clear conscience. With Your help, it's possible.

16 Hello, Mr. Mirror!

Each man should examine his own conduct for himself; then he can measure his achievement by comparing himself with himself and not with anyone else (Gal. 6:4, NEB).

Take a good look into a full-length mirror. What do you see? Does the person staring back at you need improvements? What needs to be changed? What habits should be dropped—or instituted? What about the way he reacts to others, especially in competitive business situations? How does he act or react under pressure? How does he measure up to the standards he sets for himself?

Don't waste time comparing yourself with others—especially those with lesser achievements.

Lord, when I'm through comparing myself with my ideal self, may I look long in Your direction and begin the process of upgrading all over again.

17 The Good-Evil Teeter-Totter

The purposes of the righteous are lawful;
the designs of the wicked are full of deceit
(Prov. 12:5, NEB).

Righteousness and evil are opposites. Like
weights on a teeter-totter, it sometimes appears
that evil outweighs good or vice versa. Once in
awhile it is difficult to tell the difference. It isn't
that we don't recognize righteousness, but evil is
often deceptive. That's the way the devil, the
"Deceiver," operates.

Righteousness never needs to be deceptive.
You can practice it right out in the open. And
when you do, eventually the teeter-totter will tip
in your favor.

**I know when I practice good or evil. When
I bend toward evil, transform my inner
life, O God, so others will openly see the
results!**

18 Weather Appreciation Day

As long as the world exists, there will be a time for planting and a time for harvest. There will always be cold and heat, summer and winter, day and night (Gen. 8:22, GNB).

You don't have to listen to many weathermen to know that the weather changes. God made it that way. He made the seasons, and they will continue all the days of the earth.

Cold weather will give way to warmer days. Spring, a time for sowing, will come. Summer will follow with plants in full bloom. Then comes harvest time. This cycle will never change.

Isn't it about time we stop complaining about the weather and celebrate the fact that we are alive to appreciate both rain and sunshine.

Thank You, Creator, for the weather. Help me to discover something enjoyable about every day.

19 Perfect Laws

God's laws are perfect. They protect us, make us wise, and give us joy and light (Ps. 19:7, 8, LB).

God's laws will never be found unconstitutional. These laws, especially the ones codified by Moses in the Ten Commandments, are above all other laws.

If you obey God's law to the fullest, you will experience all their benefits. There is no condemnation for the one who trusts and obeys. God's laws bring life's greatest satisfactions, fulfill life's greatest purposes, do the greatest good for the greatest number of people.

As the psalmist said, "The law of the Lord is perfect, converting the soul." Lord, grant that I shall be so transformed.

20 Do Unto Others

Don't criticize people, and you will not be criticized. For you will be judged by the way you criticize others, and the measure you give will be the measure you receive (Matt. 7:1, Phillips).

Exercising critical faculties and being critical aren't synonymous. One must make concise judgments of people, products, and principles. But criticizing, tearing others down in order to build oneself up, is dangerous.

Such an attitude opens the critic to the same treatment by others. It's like using a short ruler or a false-bottomed bushel to measure what you give. Sooner or later you can expect to be short-changed in return.

He who compliments others will also be complimented. He who cheats others will soon be cheated. He who treats others fairly will also be treated fairly.

Lord, help me to look at others the same way I want them to look at me—honestly, but kindly.

21 Love Forgets Mistakes

Love forgets mistakes; nagging about them parts the best of friends (Prov. 17:9, LB).

One comedian drew considerable laughter with this one-liner: Joy is when a nagging person falls asleep!

Who likes to hear a nagger? Nagging concentrates on life's negatives, on life's mistakes, on life's unfinished tasks. Love is positive. Love discovers the good in others and concentrates on their accomplishments rather than their mistakes. Paul said, "Love does not keep a record of wrongs."

Lord, may I be the type of person others enjoy having around. Help me to note mistakes, but not concentrate on them. Let me be keenly aware of the good others do, especially to me.

22 A New Person Altogether

You have put off the old nature with its practices and have put on the new nature, which is being renewed in knowledge after the image of its creator (Col. 3:9b-10, RSV).

Christ provides a radically different kind of life, a life that demands a new birth. Even the deeply religious Nicodemus (see John 3) had to be born again.

Paul said old things pass away and all things become new. You receive a new nature, a new personality, and the process continues. Christ wants to make all Christians more like Himself.

Thank you, Lord, for the promise that since You began the good work of making me a new person, You will keep at it until I am the way You want me to be.

23 Who Says There Is No God?

The fool says in his heart, "There is no God" (Ps. 14:1a, RSV).

"I don't believe in God!" the atheist boasts. Then he proceeds to ridicule anyone who does. He says that since no one can see, touch, hear, smell, or taste God, therefore He doesn't exist.

He doesn't realize the greatest truth about God—that He can only be discovered by faith. Thus, the psalmist calls those who hold the simplistic, atheistic view fools.

Happy are those who begin with the higher presupposition: God exists. From there one can reach out for a personal knowledge of God. That is what the Bible is all about. That is what the coming of Jesus Christ is all about. We can know God personally.

Jesus Christ, You made it possible for me not only to believe God exists, but to know Him personally. Be my defense against those who haven't come to know You yet.

24 A New Mind

Be made new in the attitude of your mind; and put on the new self, created to be like God in true righteousness and holiness (Eph. 4:23, 24, NIV).

The newness that Christian conversion produces shows up first within a person's thinking. New thought patterns develop, bringing forth new expressions, new concepts, new attitudes. We have been recreated in the likeness of Jesus Christ and that should make quite a difference in what our minds produce.

It shouldn't take long before the observing world notices a difference in us. Our mouths speak what we think, and our bodies act upon our mental commands. We become shining displays of the transforming power of Christ.

Renew my mind, O Christ. Cause me to think differently even as You think. Let me learn the meaning of "Let this mind be in you which was also in Christ."

25 The Everlasting Conflict

The righteous cannot abide an unjust man, nor the wicked a man whose conduct is upright (Prov. 29:27, NEB).

Ever notice that some evil speaking and evil acting people deliberately try to avoid you? They just can't stand having you around. Or else they call you a "holy Joe." Some think you are a religious freak.

How uncomfortable do you feel around unjust or wicked people? Don't back away from living right. Light must continue to penetrate darkness. Good must overcome evil. Righteousness must outlast wickedness. In the end it is the Christian who will hear the Lord's "Well done."

Lord, sometimes I despair when I see the prosperity of the wicked. Help me to have an eternal perspective in this changing, wicked society. Then help me to change society whenever and wherever I can.

26 Sticking Together

Ruth replied, "Don't make me leave you, for I want to go wherever you go, and to live wherever you live; your people shall be my people, and your God shall be my God" (Ruth 1:16, LB).

Family ties should be permanent. Don't fear letting these relationships be known. Stick up for one another, enjoy one another, help one another, worship together, share God with each other.

Many families split not because of disagreements but simply because of neglect. It is time to promote the idea of a big family reunion!

I'm glad I'm a part of the family of God. May Your Spirit bind me to those whom You love, and who love You.

27 Faith and Work

Trust in the Lord and do good; live in the land and be safe (Ps. 37:3, GNB).

Christianity is a vertical and horizontal religion. We are connected to God through faith in Jesus Christ. We are related to those within human society through good deeds. James referred to this as the faith/works principle. One without the other doesn't make sense.

James challenges us, "Show me how anyone can have faith without actions. I will show you my faith by my actions." This is an excellent challenge for every Christian man living today.

Lord, rather than debate how faith and works are related or contrasted, may I have the power and perseverance to demonstrate both.

28 How to Obtain Peace

He will keep in perfect peace all those who trust in him, whose thoughts turn often to the Lord! Trust in the Lord God always, for in the Lord Jehovah is your everlasting strength (Isa. 26:3, 4, LB).

Peace is a product of trust. But that trust must be in the right place—in God. No wonder most nations know so little about peace. They trust in guns, bombs, nuclear threats, and armies. Peace is never realized through the implements of war. When will we as a nation learn this?

Nor does personal peace come by dominating others. Perfect peace is an inner attitude produced through faith in God. We can leave the defense of life in His hands. Following God's laws will lead to peace with people around us.

Peace, peace! May my cries be not those of the demented person, but of one whose confidence is implanted in Him who brings peace—Christ.

29 Inner Light Glows

You are the light of the world. A city on a hill cannot be hidden. Neither do people light a lamp and put it under a bowl. Instead they put it on its stand, and it gives light to everyone in the house (Matt. 5:14, 15, NIV).

No one has ever heard of a lightless light. Candles, Edison's incandescent bulbs, fluorescent and mercury lights weren't invented to hide in some closet, but to give light. And unless the light is specifically beamed, like a flashlight or a laser beam, it will illuminate everyone and everything around.

That is the way it is when one lives for Christ. Inner light glows and gives moral direction to all around. Let your light keep on shining and don't pay too much attention to which direction its rays go. They will fall upon those who need them most.

Christ, Light of the world, shine right through me into the darkness of human society. May others be thus lighted and find the way.

30 God Is My Lawyer

You came to my rescue, Lord, and saved my life. Judge in my favor; you know the wrongs done against me (Lam. 3:58, 59, GNB).

Another translation of this verse says, "You are my lawyer." It is that type of defense we often need to deliver us from the accusations of others, from their ploys, plots, and false statements.

But God isn't limited to being attorney for the defense. He simultaneously acts as judge because He knows the wrongs done against us. And in His court we are assured of a fair trial and mercy! How great it is to personally discuss one's total case with Him.

Lord, plead my case. Be my defense. Judge accordingly. And show mercy toward those who oppose me because in love You have showed mercy toward me.

31 Ever Count Sheep?

When I call thee to mind upon my bed and think on thee in the watches of the night, remembering how thou hast been my help and that I am safe in the shadow of thy wings, then I humbly follow thee with all my heart (Ps. 63:6-8, NEB).

What do you do when you can't sleep? Count sheep? Worry about finances? Toss restlessly? Fret about how tired you'll be in the morning? Go to the refrigerator for a glass of milk? Eat cookies? Get up and read a book?

The psalmist had a better idea—he contemplated the greatness of God. Think about God's uninterrupted and stable concern for you. Think about what it means to love Him with all your heart, mind, soul, and strength. Meditate on God in those restless hours, and you'll soon be sleeping like a baby!

Spirit of God, constantly activate my mind to think about the majesty of God. Help me to use more of my waking hours for this purpose.

32 What Never to Forget

Be very careful never to forget what you have seen God doing for you. May his miracles have a deep and permanent effect upon your lives! (Deut. 4:9, LB).

It's so easy to forget. That's why most of us have appointment books. Some people tie a string around their finger. Some people put notes on a small blackboard, or else they have little magnets which hold notes on the refrigerator door. Still others keep diaries for more permanent recollection of incidents. These approaches help people remember the good things that have happened in their lives and also to make note of important events still to come.

Moses suggested we keep a diary of the acts of God on our behalf. Otherwise we might forget some of the great things He has done for us. The whole nation of Israel seemed to be afflicted with forgetfulness.

We can even copy some of the great acts of God out of His Word. Also we ought to jot down some of the things which He has done in our lives recently.

Make it happen, O Lord. Another miracle. Your glorious way of working beyond human instrumentality. Give me something to write home about and to shout out to the world.

33 Even Men Gossip

He who goes about gossiping reveals
secrets; therefore do not associate with one
who speaks foolishly (Prov. 20:19, RSV).

Gossips. They blab almost everything they
hear—in their ears and out their mouth non-
stop!

Usually gossips don't worry about accuracy
of facts. A wise person avoids the loose lipped.
But what about the subtle gossip? What do we
say to those who feel compelled to say, "I
thought you should know. . . ."

What about the person who stares back at you
in the mirror? Is he a subtle or an out-and-out
gossip? You know what to do about it!

**Lord, give me the character to keep my
mouth shut at appropriate times. May I be
one whose confidence can be trusted.**

34 Love Enemies

I [Jesus] tell you, practice loving your enemies and praying for your persecutors, to prove that you are sons of your Father in heaven . . . (Matt. 5:43, 44, Williams).

Loving your friends doesn't prove much about your character. Everybody loves friends.

But those we find difficult to like—that's a different story! It is hard to love those whose idiosyncrasies don't mesh with ours, those whose ideas and ideals are in opposition to ours, and worst of all, those who openly oppose us— enemies! Love them? Isn't that asking too much? If we have to do it with our own strength, yes. But we can draw upon the strength of Christ. Paul said, "I can do all things through Christ who strengthens me."

Lord, grant that I, like Yourself, will love people as they are, not for what they do. I remember, You loved me while I was yet a sinner—an enemy!

35 Don'ts and Do's

Happy is the man who does not take the wicked for his guide nor walk the road that sinners tread nor take his seat among the scornful (Ps. 1:12, NEB).

Once in awhile it's good to be known for the company you don't keep, or by what you don't do. So what if people laugh at your list of don'ts. You don't practice evil. You avoid health-ruining habits. You disassociate yourself from unethical people.

Of course, don't be totally negative. Let your don'ts be a good background for making a list of the things you do. And let those around you see your positive list, too.

Even though evil people prosper, Lord, give me the grace not to seek or follow their advice. Help me to choose the way of righteousness.

36 Shout It Out

Sing psalms to the Lord, for he has triumphed, and this must be made known in all the world. Cry out, and shout . . . for the Holy One of Israel is among you in majesty (Isa. 12:5, 6, NEB).

If you had an incurable disease and suddenly discovered a cure, what would you do? Keep the whole idea quiet? Never! You'd shout it out!

You know the Lord of the universe: the One who is among us in majesty, the One who has done mighty deeds, the One who has transformed your life. What have you told others about Him lately? Have you followed Isaiah's admonition to cry out and shout? He is worthy of every Christian's loudest praise and continual testimony.

Three days ago I asked for the ability to keep my mouth shut. Today I ask for ability to open it to tell how You have worked in my life, O Lord my God.

37 Being Transparent

You will never succeed in life if you try to hide your sins. Confess them and give them up; then God will show mercy to you (Prov. 28:13, GNB).

Hiding sins and faults causes insecurity. The person who does it, whether he's a small boy or a grown man, will always be afraid he'll be found out by man or by God. A clear conscience is the best foundation for confident living. Then you don't have to invent any cover- ups.

Confession makes one feel clean all the way through—so clean you are transparent. You can allow others, and even God, to look right through the depths of your thinking.

God, be merciful to me a sinner and give me the power not only to confess my wrongs but to turn from them, to give them up and go Your way.

38 Check the Stars

The heavens are telling the glory of God; they are a marvelous display of his craftsmanship. Day and night they keep on telling about God (Ps. 19:1, 2, LB).

Studying the stars should make a believer out of any thinking person. Only the egotist and fool could be an atheist. The intricacies of the universe suggest a divine planner and sustainer—an intelligent deity. Once one admits this truth, the whole universe makes a lot more sense. Our place in the universe also begins to make sense.

Listen to the universe around you. It speaks loudly about the majesty and creativity of God. Listen!

Lord, may I get the right message from the stars—not astrological nonsense, but the truth about your creative genius.

39 Measuring Greatness

Whoever would be great among you must be your servant, and whoever would be first among you must be slave of all. For the Son of man also came not to be served but to serve, and to give his life as a ransom for many (Mark 10:43, 44, RSV).

Boxer Muhammad Ali boasts, "I am the greatest." Many before him who have accomplished some feat have said the same of themselves. They expect everyone to bow, to give recognition, to serve.

The rules in Christ's arena are different. He says greatness comes by humility and by service to others, by giving of oneself. That's how Jesus became great.

Do you want the reputation of a Muhammad Ali or of Jesus Christ?

Lord, I didn't realize life would be so different when I began to follow You. Teach me what I need to learn most, to have a servant's heart and serving hands.

40 A Look at Money

If you love money, you will never be satisfied; if you long to be rich, you will never get all you want. It is useless. The richer you are, the more mouths you have to feed. All you gain is the knowledge that you are rich (Eccles. 5:10, 11, GNB).

It's great to have money. But some people never seem to have enough. They purchase life's necessities as well as life's luxuries, and still they want more. Money can never purchase ultimate happiness. It can never purchase eternal life. It can never transform the personality of the seeker.

Work hard and be satisfied with what you get. Live according to what you have, not what you hope to have. That's the most workable financial plan.

Teach me, O Christ, that the greatest riches are those of an enriched personality; that laying up treasures in heaven is life's most satisfying and challenging endeavor.

41 Think First, Speak Later

Let your conversation be always gracious, and never insipid; study how best to talk with each person you meet (Col. 4:6, NEB).

Talking off the top of one's head isn't a talent of which to be proud. Too many people display this ability, and you wish they didn't!

It's far better to be known as a thinker. Talk after mulling things over in your mind. Speak out with well-digested knowledge. Know as much as possible about the person to whom you are speaking. Then say what needs to be said rather than telling all you know. Save some of your knowledge for a future conversation. Then you'll always have something worthwhile to say when you meet your friends the next time.

Lord, help me to keep my mouth shut and my mind open. May my tongue reveal that I have something inside my head.

42 Laws Make You Free

I will live in perfect freedom, because I try
to obey your teachings (Ps. 119:45, GNB).

During the past decade a lot of Americans
began to believe that laws curb their freedom.
Consequently they have developed the concept
of obeying only the laws they think are right for
them.

This, of course, will never lead to freedom; it
will lead to anarchy. Paradoxically, obeying
laws makes one free. Those who believe that
disobedience to laws produces freedom deceive
themselves. They become slaves to disobedience.

Perfect freedom can come only in obedience
to perfect law—the teachings of the Bible. Jesus
said that if He would make you free, you would
be free indeed—free to live life to its fullest because you are free from sin, life's most enslav-
ing force.

Give me Your freedom, O Christ:
freedom from sin,
freedom from personal hangups,
freedom to be myself,
freedom to be all You desire me to be,
freedom to obey Your law.

43 Wise Politicians

Solomon prayed ". . . Give me an understanding mind so that I can govern your people well and know the difference between what is right and what is wrong. For who by himself is able to carry such a heavy responsibility?" (I Kings 3:9, LB).

Is a president or senator or governor or mayor who acknowledges his dependence upon God a weak person? By no means! True wisdom comes from God.

Fear the leader who is overwhelmingly self-confident; who disregards the principles of justice, love, and kindness; who doesn't need God.

Rejoice with those who, regardless of whether you agree with their political philosophies and legislative proposals, call upon God for wisdom. They surely will have their prayers answered and will contribute much to our society.

Lord, thank You for leaders who understand their personal limitations and know where to turn for wisdom.

44 Searching for Wisdom

If you cry out for insight and raise your voice for understanding, if you seek it like silver and search for it as for hidden treasures; then you will understand the fear of the Lord and find the knowledge of God (Prov. 2:3-5, RSV).

Wisdom doesn't grow on trees. It isn't plucked like berries from a bush. You can't get it at some special bargain sale!

Wisdom comes as the result of searching deep into oneself and into the knowledge and character of God. You don't get it like a once-in-a-lifetime vaccination. A large percentage of men don't have wisdom because they don't keep up the search.

Fear not, he who investigates, discovers; he who searches, finds; to him who knocks, it shall be opened; to him who asks, it shall be given.

God of wisdom, God of glory, give me wisdom to understand both Yourself and myself and the intellectual powers to recognize what this means for my life.

45 What Love Will Do

[Love] bears up under anything, it exercises faith in everything, it keeps up hope in everything, it gives us power to endure in anything (I Cor. 13:7, Williams).

Valentine's Day is one good time to search for the meaning of love and to express it. The true lover discovers love doesn't depend on the one being loved but on the lover. One can even love another who is sometimes obnoxious or ornery and who doesn't love back.

Love is outgoing. Beneficent thoughts and actions of the lover radiate toward the one being loved. That's why one can love enemies as well as sweethearts.

God so loved the world that He gave. Thank You for the perfect example. Imprint this attitude deep into my personality.

46 A Super Instructor

Treat me according to your constant love, and teach me your commands. I am your servant; give me understanding, so that I may know your teachings (Ps. 119:124, 125, GNB)

All of us need guidelines to follow. But sometimes even when the rules or instructions are written out we need a teacher to make them clear. Even the most complex instructions become simple when we have a teacher who shows an abundance of patience.

The child of God has such a teacher—the Holy Spirit. Jesus promised that the Spirit would teach us all things we need to know about right living and how to please God. Obedience to God's guidelines will give us abundant and everlasting life.

> **Teach me Your ways, O Lord,**
> **Teach me Your ways.**
> **Your guiding grace afford;**
> **Teach me Your ways!**

47 Mental Good Taste

Just as my mouth can taste good food, so my mind tastes truth when I hear it (Job 12:11, LB).

What man would eat a rotten apple or a spoiled orange? We spit out even the smallest bite of spoiled food.

To have the mental capacity to reject rotten ideas, moral impurities, or inferior thoughts is as great as having sensitive taste buds. Call it taste buds in the brain, if you wish. They're great to have.

To recognize good thoughts, truth, and uplifting ideas shows mental sensitivity and good taste. That marks the mentally and spiritually healthy person.

Lord, help me to think clearly, to have pure thoughts, to concentrate on truth. Lord, develop my mental and spiritual powers.

48 Being a Good Follower

So you will walk in the way of good men and keep to the paths of the righteous. For the upright will inhabit the land, and men of integrity will remain in it (Prov. 2:20, 21, RSV).

We don't like to admit it, but most of us are followers. It's the rare man who becomes a real leader.

But followers usually have something to do with the selection of leaders, and how we select leaders is of utmost importance. What do we look for? Do we observe how leaders talk? What opinion-makers believe? How our examples act?

Follow good leaders. Then take a good look over your shoulder. Someone is sure to get in line!

Jesus said, "Follow me." No better thing can I do, Lord. Give me discernment to also follow those whom You have transformed and developed into true men.

49 No Preferential Treatment

Peter began to speak: "I now realize that it is true that God treats everyone on the same basis. Whoever fears him and does what is right is acceptable to him, no matter what race he belongs to" (Acts 10:34, 35, GNB).

God has no favorite race or nation. He loves blacks, whites, Orientals. He calls Russians, Africans, Jews, and Frenchmen into His kingdom. Some from the United States and Canada also get in. No person is excluded because of where he was born or the language he utters. No person receives preferential treatment because he has money or expensive clothing. A successful businessman is treated the same as a street sweeper.

The kingdom of God is for all people everywhere. People become children of God on the basis of a heart condition, not skin color, national origin, economic status, or job rating. The sooner each of us joins Peter in this realization, the greater will be the appeal we make for others to enter the kingdom.

Thank You, Lord, for including me in Your kingdom without discriminating against my living in the Western world.

50 War or Peace

Too long have I had my dwelling among those who hate peace. I am for peace; but when I speak, they are for war! (Ps. 120:6, 7, RSV).

Build more bombers. Stockpile nuclear arms. Train bigger armies. Be ready to knock out the enemy before he is able to strike back. Fight guerilla warfare when necessary.

Headlines on TV, radio, and newspapers are dominated by war stories. A majority—or at least those in positions of power—condone war.

Is there any place for peacemakers in our world? What are we doing in the world to promote peace? Have we heard the voice of Jesus saying, "Blessed are the peacemakers"?

Somehow, my Lord, help me to maintain my religious equilibrium in a world filled with hate and war. Regardless of the odds, help me to promote that which brings peace and justice among men.

51 Bleaching One's Soul

The Lord says, "Now, let's settle the matter. You are stained red with sin, but I will wash you as clean as snow. Although your stains are deep red, you will be as white as wool" (Isa. 1:18, GNB).

The fellow who owns a laundromat would understand what we mean when we say God is in the soul-laundering business. No person can rid himself of the indelible stains of sin. But God's bleach takes out the deepest stains.

In the process God makes a person totally clean inside—like snow just after it falls or like whitened wool after a bleaching. The process involves submission to the divine launderer. If we confess our sins, He will forgive and cleanse us from all unrighteousness.

Just as I am, without one plea;
but that Your blood was shed for me,
O Lamb of God, I come, I come.

52 Keeping Your Word

People who promise things that they never give are like clouds and wind that bring no rain (Prov. 25:14, GNB).

On a hot, dry summer day a cloud appears. But the wind blows it away. The hot sun blazes down and grass and gardens wither. Hope for relief from the heat is squelched.

Have you ever been a promiser who couldn't deliver? Others thought you were just a lot of hot air.

From now on live by this principle: As much as lies within you, produce what you have promised.

God, Your promises are sure. Thank You for such faithfulness and for setting such a good example.

53 Teacher and Guide

I will teach you, and guide you in the way you should go. I will keep you under my eye (Ps. 32:8, NEB).

All of us can remember a favorite teacher. He or she usually paid particular attention to us and our problems. He or she had a distinct manner of communicating the truth of the subject being taught. Such teachers seem to be few and far between. But we remember them once they've favorably impressed us.

Christ is the great Teacher. He has distinct ways of communicating truth, of drawing something unique from each person, of nudging us in the right direction. He keeps an eye on us each day and gives us needed instruction. How can any man go wrong if he follows such a Teacher?

Lord, You are more willing to teach me than I am to be taught. May I become a more committed and responsive pupil.

54 Balanced Accounts

Abram put his faith in the Lord, and the Lord counted that faith to him as righteousness (Gen. 15:6, NEB).

Every businessman knows how difficult it can be to balance his accounts.

But what about accounts which are not financial? Some are moral, some eternal. Those which we can balance by our own genius ought so to be done. Those which require cooperation with others ought to be solved jointly.

Life's most important account requires no self-effort, just faith. It is our eternal account. The entry we make today—faith. The recorded return—righteousness. The recorder—God. The bottom line—our eternal salvation. Is your account in this balanced condition?

Not by works of righteousness which I have done, but according to Your mercy You have saved me, Lord Jesus. I accept this with deepest thanks.

55 Hungry for the Right Things

Happy are those who are hungry and thirsty for goodness, for they will be fully satisfied (Matt. 5:6, Phillips).

Were you ever so hungry that you rashly vowed you'd eat anything, just anything? Or so thirsty you didn't care whether the cup had just touched several lips before you drank from it?

When one comes to such a state in his spiritual life—parched and thirsty for God— suddenly the Lord comes with cool satisfying fulfillment.

My soul thirsts after God, yes, after the living God. I come yearningly before You, Lord. Satisfy my need.

56 Old Age Grouchiness

If a person lives to be very old, let him rejoice in every day of life, but let him also remember that eternity is far longer, and that everything down here is futile in comparison (Eccles. 11:8, LB).

I don't want to become a grouchy old man—no one does. Yet I've met too many grouches already.

A happy face, a contented heart, a positive outlook—these eliminate grouchiness and radiate the quality of life God intends for us, not only now, but for eternity. Preparing for eternity is an awesome project, but accomplishable. Do it with joy.

Help me, O God, to evaluate time on the basis of what I understand about eternity, not only quantity-wise, but quality-wise.

57 A Singular Life Goal

One thing have I asked of the Lord, that will I seek after; that I may dwell in the house of the Lord all the days of my life, to behold the beauty of the Lord, and to inquire in his temple (Ps. 27:4, RSV).

A singular life goal is difficult to formulate because we have so many pressures demanding our loyalty. How do we set priorities? What should come first in our lives? What should be our highest goal?

Is my main purpose in life to be intimately acquainted with Christ? To be more Christlike? To have some of the beauty of His personality rub off on me? To have the constant and consistent feeling that God dwells with me and I with Him? Such a lofty goal lifts life above the mundane.

Lord Jesus, You want me to be more like You. I am earthly and earthbound. Lift my eyes beyond this realm into an existence in which You are everything.

58 The Wise Use of Knowledge

Getting wisdom is the most important thing you can do. Whatever else you get, get insight. Love wisdom, and she will make you great (Prov. 4:7, 8, GNB).

Have you ever been told to "wise up"? If you have, like most people, you probably cringed a little. You didn't like the remark even though you needed it. You didn't like the remark because it carried the insinuation that you were acting foolishly.

By Solomon's standards, becoming wise is the greatest objective in life. To be able to properly and judiciously use knowledge is wisdom. It is not enough to gain more knowledge, but we must develop the ability to use knowledge in effective ways.

I pray Solomon's prayer: Lord, it isn't money or popularity I want, but wisdom. I need all I can get, all that You want to give to me.

59 Packing Each Day

What if a man should live a thousand years twice over, and never prosper? Do not both go to one place? (Eccles. 6:6, NEB).

Every four years we are given an extra day. For employees it means an extra day's pay. For employers it means extra paid wages. It also means an extra day to produce, to express our skills, to gain through mental and physical investments, to do good to others.

Sad is the person who doesn't live each day fully, who always seems to be needing another day. Sad is the person who doesn't take advantage of the time he is given, much less than a thousand years!

God, when I see others withering around me, when some die so young, teach me to number my days that I may apply my heart to wisdom and put all my mental and physical energies to work to accomplish worthwhile goals.

60 Getting At It

Be strong and courageous and get to work.
Don't be frightened by the size of the task
(I Chron. 28:20a, LB).

Okay, you've developed Christian characteristics. You've studied what the Bible says you
ought to be. You've applied these biblical truths
to your personality.

In this text David tells his son Solomon,
"You need inner character. So be strong and
courageous!" Get to work! And don't be
frightened by the size of the task. There comes a
time when the best test of whether we've developed our character is when we get off our
chairs, and even off our knees, and go to work.
That's applied biblical living.

**Lord, give me the gumption to get up and
get to work!**

61 Forward March

Every test that you have experienced is the kind that normally comes to people. But God keeps his promise, and he will not allow you to be tested beyond your power to remain firm . . . he will give you the strength to endure it (I Cor. 10:13, GNB).

At times you are tempted to follow the crowd. In many ways that is much easier than following Christ. You don't have to resist the world or defend your principles.

But you're a Christian man. You wouldn't be fully Christian if you followed the crowd. Neither would you be fully a man. So you're left with being tested.

Be of good cheer. He who got you into this Christian life will supply every means to maintain it—and to come out victoriously!

Thank You, Lord, for supplying the means of strength and the words of encouragement that make me excited about living Your way.

62 The Proof Tests

If you are weak in a crisis, you are weak indeed (Prov. 24:10, GNB).

Another translation of this verse reads, "You are a poor specimen if you can't stand the pressure of adversity."

In the working world you'll soon discover if you are weak or strong. Crises come to test your character. They reveal whether what has gone into your brain has adhered to your heart, whether biblical truth is just something you read or whether it has character-changing powers.

If you discover you are still weak in a crisis, start these meditations all over again, or at least vow to make eating soul bread a daily habit.

Lord, I'm so in need of spiritual proteins. Be my strength and keep me appropriating the strength You have already supplied.